Prickles
the Porcupine

Story by Elizabeth Russell-Arnot
Illustrations by Jenny Mountstephen

One evening,
Prickles the porcupine
crept out from underneath the leaves
where he had been sleeping all day.
He was very hungry.

Fox was nowhere to be seen,
so Prickles set off
through the forest.
He loved to eat the green leaves
that grew on the tall trees.

Prickles scurried along the ground,
and soon he came to one
of his favorite trees.

Prickles climbed up,
until he came to a long branch.
Right at the end of the branch
he could see some new green leaves.
They looked delicious!

Prickles moved carefully
along the branch.
The leaves that he wanted
seemed to be a long way out.
He had never been out this far
on a branch before.
He stopped for a minute,
and looked down.
There on the ground,
sniffing around in the dry leaves,
was Fox!

But Fox hadn't seen Prickles,
and he couldn't climb very high.

Prickles felt quite safe
up in the tree.

By now, Prickles was very hungry.
He kept crawling along the branch
toward the leaves.

But the branch was getting thinner,
and Prickles was too heavy for it.
As he moved, it started to bend.

Prickles went on very slowly.
But he still couldn't reach the leaves,
and the branch
was bending right down.

Prickles started to slip.
He tried to hang on with his claws,
but suddenly he heard a loud SNAP!
The branch was breaking!

Prickles slid off it.
He fell past small branches
and lots of leaves,
but he couldn't hang on
to any of them.
He kept falling
until he hit the ground.

Prickles lay very still
for a few minutes.
Then he stood up and shook himself.

He was not hurt,
but he had given himself a bad scare.

Just then, he heard a noise.
He looked up, and saw two eyes
shining in the moonlight.

He had forgotten about Fox!

Prickles was in great danger.
He had to think fast.
He waved his spiky tail
backward and forward.
But Fox just moved closer.

Then Prickles turned around,
and shook his tail even faster.
His hard spikes
made a rattling noise.

Fox stood quite still,
watching Prickles' tail.
Prickles moved backward.
He kept shaking his tail
from side to side.

Fox looked at the sharp spikes.
They were very close to his nose!

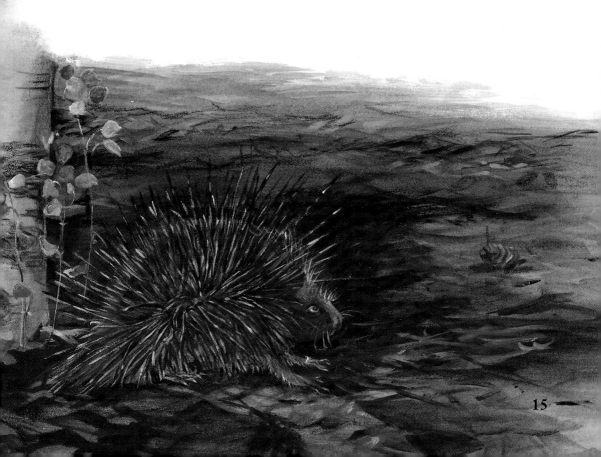

All of a sudden, Fox turned
and ran into the dark forest.

Prickles scurried back to the tree
and climbed up again.
But this time, he looked for
a wider branch to crawl along.

At last,
he was able to reach
his favorite leaves.